Liam's Big Adventure

A Day at the Beach

by Tessa Bloom

ISBN: 979-8-9945555-2-1

Illustrations by the author.
Printed in the United States of America

This is Dedicated

For the Brave Beginnings
That Lead To Many New Big Adventures

Liam is going on a Big Adventure today.

Liam is going to the beach.

He put his hat on
and his sandals.

Then he grabbed his sunglasses
and his beach bag with his towel
and his beach toys.

Mommy put Liam in his car seat and buckled his seatbelt.

Liam took his sandals off.

The sand felt funny on his toes.

The sand was warm
and very soft.

The ocean was very big and blue.

The waves were loud.

Liam stopped and watched.

“Take your time,”
Mommy said.

“I am right here.”

Liam took one small step and then another.

The water touched his toes.
It felt cold.

Liam giggled.

He splashed.
He played.

The beach wasn’t scary anymore.

The sun was shining bright.

Seagulls were flying high in the sky.

Liam built a sandcastle.

He had to reach up high to pat the top.

Liam was smiling.

“I did it!” Liam said.

“Yes, you did,” Mommy said.

“You tried something new.”

And Liam knew—

He could have many more big adventures.

About the Author

Tessa Bloom is a grandmother
who loves creating gentle stories
that help young children navigate
new experiences.
Inspired by her grandson
and the everyday bravery of little ones,
she writes picture books that offer comfort,
encouragement,
and confidence during life's first big moments.
Tessa believes that with love and reassurance,
even the scariest first days
can become meaningful adventures.

www.ingramcontent.com/pod-product-compliance
Lightning Source LLC
LaVergne TN
LVHW070205110826
845147LV00002B/505
* 9 7 9 8 9 9 4 5 5 5 5 2 1 *